Annabelle
COOKS

Annabelle COOKS

ANNABELLE WHITE

PENGUIN BOOKS

Contents

Introduction	9
Breakfast	10
Coffee Break	16
Lunch	24
Barbecues	42
Family Dinners	56
Desserts & Baking	68
Spreads & Dressings	78
Index	80

PENGUIN BOOKS

Penguin Books (NZ) Ltd,
cnr Airborne and Rosedale Roads,
Albany, Auckland 1310,
New Zealand

Penguin Books Ltd,
27 Wrights Lane,
London W8 5TZ, England

Penguin Putnam Inc,
375 Hudson Street,
New York, NY 10014,
United States

Penguin Books Australia Ltd,
487 Maroondah Highway,
Ringwood, Australia 3134

Penguin Books Canada Ltd,
10 Alcorn Avenue, Toronto,
Ontario, Canada M4V 3B2

Penguin Books (South Africa) Pty Ltd,
5 Watkins Street, Denver Ext 4,
2094, South Africa

Penguin Books India (P) Ltd,
11, Community Centre,
Panchsheel Park,
New Delhi 110 017, India

Penguin Books Ltd,
Registered Offices:
Harmondsworth,
Middlesex, England

First published by Penguin Books (NZ) Ltd,
1999

10 9 8 7 6 5 4 3 2 1

Copyright © Annabelle White 1999

The right of Annabelle White to be identified as the author of this work in terms of section 96 of the Copyright Act 1994 is hereby asserted.

Designed by emdesign

Typeset by Seven

Photography by Kieran Scott

Printed by Wyatt & Wilson Print, Christchurch

All rights reserved. Without limiting the rights under copyright reserved above, no part of this publication may be reproduced, stored in or introduced into a retrieval system, or transmitted, in any form or by any means (electronic, mechanical, photocopying, recording or otherwise), without the prior written permission of both the copyright owner and the above publisher of this book.

Acknowledgements

First, a huge thank you to the two people who helped me produce this book: chef Nicola Hudson for being the ultimate assistant—from re-testing recipes, styling the most beautiful plates and maintaining great enthusiasm for this project from start to finish, and photographer Kieran Scott for capturing on film the delightful simplicity, ease and appeal of these dishes. Thank you both.

Many thanks to Gourmet Direct for superb lamb and salmon, to Chubby Chicken for top-quality chicken, and Mainland for supplying all the great products we needed for this book.

A very special thank you to Bruce Campbell and the team at Mainland, to John McDonald and the crew at '5.30 With Jude', to Steve Barnett and the staff at Penguin, and Paul Brockett at Fisher & Paykel.

No book of mine would be complete without a mention of the support and assistance given from Lloyd Anderson, Penny Pearson and my willing samplers from close friends to neighbours, including my parents, John and Jacqueline White.

Thank you all.

*"To my Aunty Alice,
who for years has inspired me with
her enthusiasm and results in the kitchen.
Her culinary efforts are mixed with love, humour
and thoughtfulness; everyone should have
an Aunty Alice."*

Introduction

Culinary feedback is my greatest joy. When approached by fellow cooks standing at the bus stop, or when receiving cards and letters at work expressing delight at a recipe, it energises me to do more.

Working with the '5.30 With Jude' team has completely revolutionised this contact with fellow foodies. For ten years I have worked as a food writer in print and have had lovely mail, but when you appear on television you become part of the family. There you are stirring away, looking red-faced (but enthusiastic) in the kitchen just before the news, and viewers respond positively to simple, economical dishes with great ingredients.

Such is my spot with Mainland Products on television and such is the support and interest for the recipes that we decided to collate them as well as provide you with some new suggestions. This book is the end result.

I have dedicated this book to my Aunty Alice, because she is the best example of an inspiring country cook I have ever met. She bottles, preserves, bakes with gusto, makes the lightest sponges out of farm eggs, prepares the best neenish tarts (my brother in LA asks for them whenever he visits), collects whitebait or shellfish to make fritters, whips up dinners and lunches with ease and prepares legendary afternoon teas.

Waking up at her farm in Nukuhou North in the Bay of Plenty we were treated to breakfast in bed with a beautifully presented tray and perfectly cooked breakfast, including freshly squeezed juice.

This commitment to country hospitality left a lasting impression on me. Anyone with such energy for doing things with style and celebrating food at such an early hour is an inspiration and needs to be acknowledged. So, Aunty Alice, this book is for you.

Enjoy this collection of delicious recipes and, most important of all, use this book. The family will be delighted when it looks battered and worn!

Annabelle White

P.S. If you are thinking of popping in and having a cup of tea and a chance to sample Aunty Alice's largesse, unfortunately she has retired and moved into town.

Fruit and Banana Smoothie

2 cups cold milk
1 banana
500 g berry fruit yoghurt

Place the first 2 ingredients in the blender and process. Add the yoghurt after the banana has been blended through the milk.

Serve.

I add Naturalea herbal echinacea, blackcurrant & honey yoghurt to give an intensity of fruit flavours as well as helping the immune system!

Try adding 2 tablespoons passionfruit syrup (minus seeds) to a fruit smoothie with low-fat milk, yoghurt and a banana. Serve with a sprig of mint.

Pawpaw Smoothie

¼ pawpaw, seeded and diced
1 cup low-fat milk
3 Tbsp natural yoghurt
2 fresh apricots or 4 apricot halves (canned)

Place all the ingredients in the blender and process until smooth.

* Pawpaw is great for the digestive system—this is a great excuse to improve your health!

Fruit Salad Smoothie

1 cup fruit juice
1 banana, chopped
1 orange, peeled
½ cup milk
3–4 Tbsp berry fruit yoghurt

Place the fruit juice, banana and orange segments into the blender. Process well and add the remaining ingredients. Give an additional whirl and serve.

Spirulina Smoothie

1 cup cold low-fat milk
1 banana
½ cup low-fat yoghurt
⅓ cup pineapple juice
1 Tbsp spirulina powder

Place the first 3 ingredients in the blender and process well. Add the next 2 ingredients and process further. Note: Spirulina powder is always best added as the last ingredient to a smoothie.

You can add a tablespoon of wheat germ if desired. Smoothies are a fun, healthy approach to breakfast for the super-fast, who want great flavour and health benefits on the go!

Experiment with different flavours of yoghurt, milk and fruit.

(left to right) Fruit and Banana Smoothie; Pawpaw Smoothie; Spirulina Smoothie

Camembert Omelette

Add thin wedges of room-temperature camembert to the omelette and serve with grilled breakfast sausages for a substantial and tasty brunch.

**A knob of butter or 1 Tbsp oil
2 large eggs
2 Tbsp cream
Salt and pepper
4 thin wedges of camembert**

Place the knob of butter or oil in a well-greased or non-stick pan. In a small bowl lightly beat the eggs, cream and seasoning. Do not over-beat or the mixture will be tough. Pour the omelette into the pan and make sure the mixture covers the complete cooking surface. Turn down the heat and work quickly. Draw the edges with a fork to allow the uncooked egg to run underneath. When the base is golden brown, place the camembert on top of the egg mixture and place under a hot grill for a few seconds. When the cheese begins to soften, flip one side over onto the other. Serve immediately.

If you have fresh parsley or chives in the garden they will make a delightful addition to your omelette.

If you have cold roast or steamed potato in the fridge, dice and add to the hot pan with the butter and cook till golden on either side. If necessary, add more eggs and a little water to bind the potato together. Cooked potatoes and eggs are a stunning combination!

Serve with slow-baked tomatoes topped with pesto. Place tomatoes in a slow oven with a drizzle of oil for hours! Top with pesto.

John's Fruit and Nut Porridge

On a crisp, clear mid-winter morning in glorious Queenstown my great friend John loves to whip up this hearty porridge for breakfast for guests at his Evergreen Lodge.

Serves 4
**1 cup rolled oats
½ cup oatmeal*
¼ cup sultanas
2 Tbsp liquid honey
2 Tbsp milk powder
¼ cup chopped dried apricots
¼ cup slivered almonds
¼ cup roughly chopped walnuts
Pinch salt
3–4 cups milk**

Topping:
**2 bananas, sliced
25 g butter
2 Tbsp chopped walnuts
4 Tbsp brown sugar**

Mix all the porridge ingredients together, except the milk, in a large microwave-proof bowl. When blended, add the milk, cover and microwave for 2–3 minutes on high. Stir, then microwave for a further 4 minutes. Leave to rest for a minute while you prepare the bananas.

Toss the bananas, walnuts and brown sugar in the melted butter.

Serve the porridge in bowls and top with the banana mixture. Serve with more milk or cream.

*To make oatmeal just place rolled oats in a food processor and process into a fine powder.

Camembert Omelette

Crisp Potato Cake served with Bacon and Eggs

Serves 4 with 2 cakes each

Potato Cakes
6 medium old potatoes
Salt
Oil to sauté
4 Tbsp finely chopped chives or parsley
Salt and pepper to season
Flour to bind (if needed)
12 rashers bacon, grilled

Peel the potatoes, place in a medium saucepan and boil till just tender. Drain and cool.

Grate the cooled potatoes into a bowl. Add chives or parsley to potato. Season and roll into patties with your hands. If mixture is too wet or sloppy, add flour to bind your cakes.

Fry in a shallow pan of oil till golden brown. Allow 3–5 minutes each side—keep the sauté pan on a medium heat as you want your potato cakes to be sizzling but not catching!

To assemble: Place 2 potato cakes on a plate with the grilled bacon rashers alongside. Top with a poached egg or with softly scrambled eggs.

Apricot Buttermilk Muffins

Makes 12 large muffins

2½ cups flour
1 Tbsp baking powder
¼ tsp salt
2 large eggs
⅓ cup sugar
250 ml (1 cup) buttermilk
140 g butter, melted
2 tsp vanilla
425 g fresh apricots, finely chopped
½ cup pecan nuts, finely chopped
1 tsp ground cinnamon

Preheat oven to 200°C. Sift flour, baking powder and salt into a large bowl. In a separate bowl whisk together the eggs, sugar, buttermilk, melted butter and vanilla. Return the dry ingredients to the sieve and sift them onto the egg mixture. Fold dry ingredients quickly into the wet mixture. Do not beat or stir—the mixture does have an uneven appearance.

Gently fold in the apricots, pecan nuts and cinnamon. Place in greased muffin trays and top with cinnamon topping.

Cinnamon Topping
1 Tbsp butter, melted
⅓ cup raw sugar
2 tsp cinnamon
Additional pecan nuts

Combine all the ingredients and place a dash on top of each muffin, then top with half a pecan nut.

Bake at 200°C for 20–25 minutes.

You can avoid double sifting if desired, but sifting twice means that mixing time is kept to a minimum. This is very desirable when making top-quality muffins.

You can use canned unsweetened apricots for this recipe—just drain apricots and chop up finely—425 g is approximately 1¼ cups.

Crisp Potato Cake served with Bacon and Eggs

Easy Bran Muffins

The great feature of these muffins is that you can make the mix up and store it in the fridge for up to a week.

Makes 24–30

3 cups bran
1 cup boiling water
2 large eggs, lightly beaten
1 cup ginseng apricot and vanilla yoghurt
1 cup milk
½ cup melted butter or ½ cup salad oil
1 cup fruit (a mixture of sultanas, diced banana and diced apricots works well)
2½ tsp baking soda
½ tsp salt
½ cup brown sugar
1½ cups flour
1 cup wholemeal flour

In a large bowl mix the bran with boiling water and set aside to cool. Add eggs, yoghurt, milk, melted butter or salad oil, sultanas, diced banana and chopped apricots.

In a separate bowl, stir together baking soda, salt, sugar and flours. Blend thoroughly and stir into bran mixture.

To store, refrigerate batter in a tightly covered container for up to 1 week.

Bake at 220°C for 15–20 minutes.

Spinach and Feta Muffins

This recipe comes from my good friend and great cook Julie Clark. She created these delicious muffins for her busy café in the Wellington Library. There never needs to be an excuse to eat spinach and feta—they are a partnership in heaven!

200 ml vegetable oil
1 egg
2 cups milk
2 cups raw spinach (compacted)
600 g or 4⅔ cups plain flour
½ tsp ground nutmeg
½ tsp black pepper (ground)
½ tsp salt
4 tsp baking powder
150 g diced feta

Preheat the oven to 190°C fan bake or 200°C regular bake.

Put the oil, egg, milk and spinach in a food processor and process until finely chopped. In a separate bowl, mix the dry ingredients together. Fold through the feta until coated. Add the spinach mix and combine. Place in greased muffin pans and fan bake at 190°C for approximately 25 minutes.

These muffins are delicious with chopped sundried tomatoes, finely chopped spring onion, capsicum or even finely diced eggplant.

Spinach and Feta Muffins

Fruit-filled Buttermilk Scones

Banana-Nut Loaf

This is simply delicious fresh from the oven. Serve a slice with coffee, with or without butter according to your taste. I recommend a lemon or other citrus icing if you enjoy icing on a loaf.

⅓ cup sour cream
1 tsp baking soda
125 g butter, at room temperature
1 cup sugar
2 large eggs
1 cup mashed banana (2 small or 1 large)
2 cups flour
½ tsp baking powder
½ cup chopped walnuts or almonds

Preheat the oven to 180°C. Grease a 22 cm x 12 cm loaf tin or spray with oil spray. Combine the sour cream and baking soda in a small bowl. Using an electric mixer, cream the butter and sugar in a large bowl. Beat in eggs, bananas and sour cream mixture. Sift in flour and baking powder. Stir in nuts. Spoon mixture into prepared tin. Bake for 1 hour or until a skewer comes cleanly from the loaf. Cool 10 minutes in the pan. Turn the loaf out onto a rack and cool completely.

Fruit-filled Buttermilk Scones

Forget dry scones and whip up a batch of these sensational ones —buttermilk makes them light, tangy and ever so moist. Buttermilk is a cook's secret weapon and very user-friendly! This recipe makes 15 scones.

3 cups flour
Pinch of salt
2 heaped tsp baking powder
60 g butter
1½ cups buttermilk
1 cup dried fruit (currants and chopped apricots work well)

Preheat the oven to 220°C. Place the flour, salt and baking powder in the food processor and whirl together. Add the butter (in pieces, not whole) and when the mixture is fully integrated and resembles fine breadcrumbs you are ready to add the buttermilk. Shake the buttermilk.

Place the flour/butter mixture into a large bowl and with a knife add the buttermilk with the dried fruit. Keep the mixture wet. Add more buttermilk if necessary.

Place the mixture on a floured bench and gently pat out into shape with a quick knead (about 6 times only). Cut into pieces and place on a baking tray, close together.

Bake at 220°C for 15–18 minutes.

Serve these light and moist scones with butter and jam.

Tararua buttermilk was used for all of our buttermilk recipes.

Chocolate and Coconut Sour Cream Loaf

This is deliciously moist and full flavoured; ideal to serve with morning coffee.

2 large eggs
¼ cup oil (not olive)
1 cup sugar
250 g sour cream
1½ cups flour
1½ tsp baking powder
1 tsp baking soda
¼ tsp salt

Chocolate and Coconut Mix
¼ cup coconut
½ cup grated dark chocolate

Beat the eggs until they are frothy. Beat in the oil and sugar, then add the sour cream and other ingredients. Grease a large loaf tin and place half the batter in it. Sprinkle half the coconut and two-thirds of the chocolate evenly over the batter. Add the remaining batter and sprinkle the rest of the coconut and chocolate on top.

Cut through the mixture with a knife for a marbling effect.

Bake at 180°C for 55–60 minutes. Let the loaf stand for 10 minutes, then turn out.

Blueberry Cheesecake Brownies

Serve small pieces of these brownies. They are quite delicious and disappear quickly.

200 g dark cooking chocolate, chopped
125 g butter
1 cup sugar
3 large eggs
1 tsp vanilla
¾ cup flour

Cheesecake Topping
250 g cream cheese, softened
½ cup sugar
2 tsp fresh lemon juice
1 large egg
½ tsp vanilla
¼ tsp salt
2 Tbsp flour
1½ cups blueberries (frozen are fine, just defrost and drain)
Icing sugar to sprinkle for garnish, if desired

Preheat the oven to 180°C. Butter and flour a 33 cm x 22 cm baking pan.

Make the brownie: In a metal bowl set over a pan of barely simmering water melt the chocolate with the butter, stirring, then cool. Whisk in the sugar and eggs, one at a time, and whisk in vanilla. Whisk in flour until just combined and spread the mix evenly in the prepared pan.

Make cheesecake topping: In a bowl with an electric mixer cream together the cream cheese and sugar until light and fluffy. Beat in lemon juice, egg, vanilla and salt. Beat in flour and spread mixture evenly over the brownie batter.

Scatter the blueberries over the topping and sprinkle with sugar.

Bake in the middle of the oven for 35–40 minutes or until the top is puffed and pale golden and a tester comes out with crumbs adhering to it. Do not over-cook.

Cool brownies completely in the pan on a rack and chill, covered, at least 6 hours or overnight. Dust with icing sugar if desired. Makes 20 brownies.

(top to bottom) Blueberry Cheesecake Brownies; Chateau Yering Tea Cakes (see recipe on page 74); Chocolate and Coconut Sour Cream Loaf

Mini Cheese Muffins

Cheese puffs are part of the New Zealand tradition of baking. These muffins are a variation on the same theme and make a great economical addition to your next drinks party. Taking pantry ingredients, plus some milk and cheese and an egg from the fridge, you have these taste sensations!

Makes 36 small muffins

1 egg
¼ tsp salt
¼ cup olive oil
2 cups flour
4 tsp baking powder
2 cups grated tasty cheddar cheese
2 Tbsp chopped parsley
½ cup cooked bacon, finely chopped
1½ cups milk
Extra cheese for garnishing (I used 100 g blue vein, crumbled)

Lightly beat the egg, salt and olive oil and place to one side. Sift flour and baking powder into a large bowl. Mix cheese, parsley and bacon bits into the flour mixture. Make a well in the centre and add the egg mixture and the milk. Mix together gently—do not over-mix. Spoon into small muffin tins and sprinkle with extra cheese.

Bake at 190°C until golden brown—allow 15–18 minutes.

Once cooked, turn out of tins and cover with a cloth.

When these muffins have cooled, slit them three-quarters open and place a small slice of brie inside the muffin. Reheat in a hot oven till the cheese melts—this will only take a few minutes and you will have an irresistible nibble for your friends and family.

Delicious Orange Sour Cream Cake

In a word—divine!

250 g softened butter
2 cups sugar
6 eggs, lightly beaten
4 tsp finely grated orange rind
2 cups flour
2 tsp baking powder
1 cup (250 g) sour cream

Glaze
Juice of 1 orange and ¼ cup sugar (combined together)

Cream the butter and sugar until light and fluffy. Add the eggs and orange rind and blend well.

Fold in flour and baking powder alternately with the sour cream. Mix gently until smooth and pour into a well-greased 26 cm spring-bottom round tin. Bake at 160°C for 60-80 minutes or until a skewer comes out cleanly when tested.

After baking leave this cake in the tin for a few minutes, then pour on the glaze. Leave for another few minutes and then remove from the pan.

Serve with whipped cream and fresh orange curd.

Delicious Orange Sour Cream Cake

Blue Cheese and Parsnip Soup

The secret to this soup combination is the addition of some crumbled blue vein cheese in the base of the soup plate before adding the hot soup. If you prefer, you can serve the room-temperature blue cheese on croutes or small toasts.

Serves 4–6

1 large onion
3 cloves garlic
Olive oil
1 Tbsp curry powder
6 medium parsnips, peeled and finely sliced
5½ cups chicken stock
Salt and pepper to taste
Fresh chopped parsley to garnish
¼ cup cream or milk
2 100 g wedges blue vein cheese

Cook the onion and garlic in a little olive oil until soft. Add the curry powder and the peeled and finely sliced parsnips. Sweat for 5 minutes, making sure the parsnips do not catch, then add the chicken stock. Bring to the boil and simmer for 30–45 minutes. Adjust the seasonings. Purée, then add the freshly chopped parsley and cream just prior to serving.

Crumble the blue vein cheese into the bowls, allowing 1 wedge for 2–3 bowls of soup. Pour the hot soup into the bowl. Top with parsley and serve.

If you have additional cream, you can also swirl a little over the edge of the melting cheese for an extra bonus if desired.

This soup is also delicious using pumpkin, cauliflower or broccoli instead of parsnip.

Root Vegetable Mash

150 g peeled potatoes
150 g peeled kumara
100 g parsnip
100 g carrot
½ peeled and roughly chopped onion
100 g butter
Salt and pepper to season
A spoonful of crème fraîche

Cook the peeled vegetables in a large pot of salted water. When cooked, drain and add the butter and season with salt and pepper. To make it extra luscious, add a spoonful of crème fraîche to the mixture.

Blend until smooth. Check seasoning. Place in a clean pot, add a knob of butter and heat gently.

Serve with beef fillet, grilled fish, roast chicken or even the humble grilled sausage.

If it's beef, make a super-simple mustard sauce to accompany the mash and beef. Heat 150 ml cream in a saucepan with 2–3 tablespoons grain mustard—allow to simmer to desired consistency. Add black pepper for seasoning, if required.

Blue Cheese and Parsnip Soup

Leek Fondue

This recipe is so simple you will think we have made a mistake. It has only four ingredients and can be made quickly to serve with roasted chicken or beef, grilled fish or even grilled sausages. The recipe was given to me by top Auckland chef Glenn Dentice.

80 g butter
1 bunch leeks, whites only, finely sliced
3 Tbsp white wine
100 ml (approximately ½ cup) crème fraîche
Salt and freshly ground black pepper

In a pan heat 20 g of butter and toss in the leeks. Stir for a few minutes, then add the white wine. Add the crème fraîche and keep stirring. Cook for a few minutes to thicken, then add the remaining butter.

Cook slowly for about 20 minutes until the leeks are very tender.

Season with salt and pepper.

Here's another great crème fraîche suggestion from Glenn: Melt 300 g butter in a frypan. Add 150 g tomato purée, ¼ teaspoon cayenne pepper and 1 tablespoon dried tarragon leaves. When the mixture is simmering add a 250 g pottle of crème fraîche. Season. This is a rich sauce but served lightly with grilled fish it's delicious. Serve with a green salad.

Chilled Cucumber, Avocado and Yoghurt Soup

On a hot summer's day an evening meal or lunch under the trees is particularly elegant with a bowl of chilled soup. Chilled soups in the summer are as restorative as a bowl of hearty soup in winter. Cold, sensual, palate cleansing, healthy and just plain delicious—make up a batch and try it for yourself.

Serves 4
1 large cucumber, peeled and roughly chopped
2 avocados, peeled and roughly chopped
Juice of 1 lemon
1 tsp crushed garlic
1 tsp finely chopped mint
1 tsp finely chopped parsley
1 Tbsp Thai sweet chilli sauce
2 cups plain yoghurt
Salt to season
Extra water to mix

Put all the ingredients into the food processor and mix until smooth. Store in fridge, covered, until ready to serve.

Garnish with a small spoonful of sour cream and a sprig of mint.

Chilled Cucumber, Avocado and Yoghurt Soup

Impossible-to-Fail Quiche

Courgette Cheese Pie

This simple, fast recipe enhances the courgette and makes good use of pantry staples. With a block of tasty cheddar cheese in the fridge, some courgettes from the garden and a packet of baking mix from the supermarket, you can whip this up in seconds.

Serves 6–8

½ **cup grated cheddar cheese**
3 **cups grated courgettes**
1 **cup baking mix**
½ **cup oil**
2 **Tbsp chopped parsley**
4 **large eggs**
Salt and pepper to taste

Mix the cheese, courgettes, baking mix, oil and parsley together in a large bowl. In a smaller bowl, beat the eggs and seasoning. Add to the larger bowl and pour into a greased 23 cm pie plate. Bake at 190°C for 40 minutes.

Cut into wedges.

Serve this with a tossed salad and crunchy bread.

Even if your family members are not keen on courgettes they may still enjoy this pie—one member of my family who protests at the sight of courgettes loves this pie. He is never too sure what exactly is in it!

You could add sundried tomatoes and, if desired, mix cheddar and feta together. Just take care with the seasoning if you are using feta, you won't need extra salt.

Impossible-to-Fail Quiche

This economical and easy recipe is a superb vehicle to show the delicious flavours of an aged cheddar cheese. A full-flavoured aged cheese transports a simple egg and cheese dish into something quite memorable!

3 **eggs**
½ **cup self-raising flour**

1 **cup aged cheddar cheese, grated**
1 **Tbsp oil**
1¼ **cups milk**
1 **onion, finely chopped**
2 **rashers bacon, rind removed (optional), chopped**

Place all the ingredients except the bacon into a large bowl or other container, or a large food processor bowl, and either stir or shake with vigour for 1 minute or process for 30 seconds.

Pour into a hot, greased quiche dish and add bacon and anything else you think would work—a few tablespoons of chopped parsley, and/or corn, and/or raw mushrooms—just clean out the fridge!

Bake 180°C for 45 minutes.

Serve with a salad and a bowl of crusty bread.

Mainland vintage cheddar works well with this family favourite.

Vietnamese Chicken Salad

This super-simple salad is so popular with my friends and family that I get requests to serve it, after loud hints about the need for more great Asian flavours in our daily diet.

Serves 4–6

2 chicken breast fillets
Peanut oil
150 g mesclun salad mix
½ telegraph cucumber, seeded and sliced
2–3 Tbsp finely chopped mint
70 g (½ cup) roasted chopped cashew nuts
½ red capsicum, thinly sliced
425 g tin mango slices or 1 fresh mango

Dressing
¼ cup Thai sweet chilli sauce
1½ Tbsp rice vinegar
2 tsp lemon juice
1 Tbsp fish sauce
Black pepper to taste
Sugar to taste (optional)

For dressing, combine all ingredients with 1½ tablespoon water, season to taste and mix well.

Place chicken on oven tray, brush with peanut oil and grill for 6–7 minutes each side, or until cooked. Rest in a warm place for 5 minutes, then cut lengthwise into thin pieces.

Add chicken to remaining ingredients and mix to combine. Pour dressing over and toss gently.

Salads like this look splendid on large white platters. Do not fuss with the presentation—just combine together and serve straightaway.

You can't substitute the fish sauce or the rice vinegar—check your local supermarket first and then try an Asian supply store.

Chicken, Brie and Bacon Salad

There is something quite magical about eating a crisp salad with chicken, bacon, avocado and pine nuts with your favourite garlic-herb dressing. Yum!

Serves 6

8 cups salad greens
6 cups cooked smoked chicken, in bite-sized chunks
1 red onion, finely sliced into rings
1 brie, at room temperature and cut into wedges
6 rashers bacon, rind removed, cut into strips
½ cup toasted pine nuts (optional)

Place the washed and prepared salad greens on a large platter. Scatter the chicken meat, red onion, brie slices and freshly grilled bacon over the platter of salad greens in that order.

Drizzle with salad dressing and top with pine nuts for extra crunch.

Add 2–3 cups seedless grapes to this salad if desired. At Christmas you could replace the smoked chicken with roast turkey and perhaps add fresh mango or pawpaw as well.

Chicken, Brie and Bacon Salad

Double Cream Camembert and Chicken Crêpes

With a camembert in the fridge and a few leftovers you can make a very smart dinner within minutes!

Crêpes
1 cup flour
2 large eggs
½ tsp salt
1 cup milk
1 Tbsp oil or melted butter

Filling
115 g (½) double cream camembert
1 cup cooked rice
1 cup cooked diced chicken
1 cup finely sliced mushrooms
¼ cup chopped parsley
2–3 chopped spring onions
½ cup toasted pine nuts
Salt and pepper

Topping
1 cup grated aged cheddar (I used Mainland cheddar Master's Vintage cheese)

Crêpes: Place all the ingredients in a blender or food processor and whirl until well blended. Leave to stand for 1 hour. Make crêpes and place a few tablespoons of the filling in the centre and roll up. Place in a greased dish and top with grated cheese. Bake at 180°C for 30–40 minutes.

Filling: Cut the camembert into pieces and combine in a large bowl with the remaining ingredients.

Blue Cheese Vegetable and Bacon Tarts

A superb reworking of a bacon and egg pie. Add vegetables and blue cheese and transform a beloved Kiwi classic into a memorable lunch.

Serves 6
1 red onion, chopped
1 large clove garlic, chopped
2 Tbsp butter
500 g peeled pumpkin, par-cooked
60 g spinach
45 g broccoli, par-cooked
250 g crusty pie pastry
100 g blue cheese
4 rashers middle bacon
2 large eggs
1 cup cream
Milk for pastry glazing

Sweat the onion and garlic in butter. Slice and pre-cook the vegetables.

Roll the pastry and place in individual 8 cm tartlet tins. Place all the vegetables in the uncooked pie shells. Crumble the blue cheese over the vegetables.

Remove the rind from the bacon and with kitchen scissors, or a sharp knife, finely chop the bacon into small pieces. Place the bacon pieces over the top of the cheese in the pie cases. Beat the eggs and cream together and pour over the cheese, vegetables and bacon in each tin.

Brush the pastry edges with milk. Bake at 180°C until golden. Allow 20–25 minutes.

Blue Cheese Vegetable and Bacon Tarts

Antipasto

One of the simplest means of entertaining a group of people is to get together and share an antipasto platter. Antipasto literally means 'before pasta', so anything goes from chunks of salami to gherkins, from beer sticks to slices of pastrami, from slices of cheese to sundried tomatoes.

For our antipasto we used cubed feta, diced salami, sliced pastrami, sundried tomatoes, olives, grilled frankfurters, fresh basil, caper berries, char-grilled vegetables and Turkish bread. The warm, moist bread is the perfect partner for these delicacies, and char-grilled vegetables are always popular.

Char-grilled Vegetables

1 small eggplant, sliced
1 courgette, seeded and sliced on an angle
1 red capsicum, seeded and sliced
1 yellow capsicum, seeded and sliced
Salt for seasoning
Olive oil for spraying
1 cup olive oil
1 tsp salt
1 tsp chopped parsley
2 tsp crushed garlic
Crushed pepper
1 Tbsp lemon juice

Season the vegetables with salt and spray with oil. Place on a char-grill until marked. When cool place in a bowl with the olive oil, salt, chopped parsley, crushed garlic, crushed pepper and lemon juice.

Turkish Bread

This is the most delicious bread to make on the barbecue. Perfect as part of the antipasto platter and designed for that 'easy hour or so' before the barbecue cooking is seriously undertaken.

Makes 6 pieces
1½ tsp dried yeast
160 ml tepid water
250 g (about 2 cups) plain flour
½ tsp salt
1 clove garlic, crushed
2 tsp mixed herbs
Olive oil
Rock or sea salt

Dissolve the yeast in tepid water. Combine the flour, salt, crushed garlic and mixed herbs and add the yeast mixture once it is foaming—allow 20 minutes. Mix and place in a bowl with a slight layer of olive oil.

Cover with a clean cloth and place in a warm spot to prove. Allow approximately 2 hours.

Divide into 6 pieces. Roll out and shape as desired. Brush with olive oil. Place on a char-grill or barbecue and cook for approximately 3 minutes each side. Sprinkle with sea salt while cooking.

Serve immediately.

Antipasto

Easy Tuna Flan

Many years ago my mother started making this flan and it has been a family favourite ever since. Serve it warm with a mixed green salad. Try adding thin slices of capsicums to the salad—they work well with this flan.

Serves 6
2 180 g cans tuna, drained
½ cup chopped spring onions
350 g crusty pie pastry or similar
3 eggs
1 cup cottage cheese with chives
¼ cup milk
Salt and pepper to taste

Combine the tuna and chopped spring onions. Line a 23 cm flan dish with pastry and place tuna mixture in the bottom.

Beat the eggs until frothy. Combine the cottage cheese, milk and seasoning and beat until combined. Fold into the eggs and mix well. Pour egg mixture over the tuna. Bake for 1 hour at 190°C. Serve warm.

Delicious Flan Pastry

120 g butter
120 g cream cheese
1 cup plain flour

Cream the butter and cream cheese together and beat thoroughly. Add flour and blend with a fork till a ball forms and no more. Never over-work pastry—the less you do the better. Wrap in plastic wrap and refrigerate for 1 hour. Roll out to fit a 20–23 cm pie plate.

Chicken Parmesan

Chicken is ever-popular at lunch. Serve these with fresh bread rolls and a salad. They can be the base for a great hearty chicken sandwich if desired. Versatile and flexible, this tasty treatment of chicken will delight.

500–750 g boneless, skinless chicken breast halves
½ cup buttermilk
2 Tbsp grated parmesan cheese
1 Tbsp plus 1 tsp flour
¾ cup seasoned breadcrumbs
2 Tbsp olive oil
2–3 cloves garlic, crushed

Place the chicken between 2 sheets of waxed paper and pound lightly with a mallet or other heavy flat object to flatten to about 6 mm (¼ inch). Combine buttermilk and parmesan in a bowl. Dust chicken with flour mixed with salt and pepper to taste. Dip both sides of chicken in buttermilk mixture. Place breadcrumbs on a piece of wax paper. Dredge both sides of chicken in breadcrumbs. Heat oil in a heavy non-stick frypan over medium-high heat. Sauté garlic for 1 minute. Discard the garlic and sauté the chicken for 4–5 minutes or until golden. Turn and sauté for another 3–4 minutes or until browned and chicken is cooked throughout.

Easy Tuna Flan

Fuss-free Lemon Cheesecake

Maple Syrup Glazed Pears

These pears are a delicious partner to a cheese board. Place your 3 favourite cheeses on a large white platter and serve at room temperature for the perfect finale to a meal. A blue cheese, a brie or camembert and an aged cheddar is always a safe starting point.

5–6 pears
Melted butter
1 cup whole walnuts
¼ cup maple syrup (approximately)

Turn on your oven grill. Seed and quarter pears, but do not peel. Place on a grilling tray and brush with melted butter. Place the walnuts at one end of the tray and slowly drizzle a little maple syrup over the nuts and pears.

Place under the grill. The cooking process takes only a few minutes, so stay by the oven—any movement away will result in burnt fruit and nuts!

After 4–5 minutes (depending on the intensity of your oven) the nuts will have coloured. Remove from the tray and allow to cool. They will appear sticky, but will harden on cooling. Return the pears to the grill for a few more minutes, no longer. They should still have a firm texture to accompany the cheese.

Place on the cheese board in clusters.

If you can't access real maple syrup for this recipe you could drizzle a little liquid honey onto the pears and the walnuts. If the honey is quite thick, just add a little hot water and blend through before drizzling.

Fuss-free Lemon Cheesecake

250 g pkt round wine biscuits
125 g melted butter
250 g traditional cream cheese
1 cup castor sugar
1 tsp vanilla
¼ cup lemon juice (no pips)
85 g pkt lemon jelly
¾ cup boiling water
1 cup evaporated milk, well chilled
1 cup cream

Make the usual biscuit base: Crush the wine biscuits in a food processor and combine with the melted and cooled butter. Press half-way up the sides of a loose-based cake tin. Chill. Into a large mixing bowl put the room-temperature cream cheese, castor sugar, vanilla and lemon juice and squash it all with a potato masher or blend in a food processor until smooth.

Make a jelly with the boiling water. Cool and then add to the cream cheese mixture. In another bowl beat the evaporated milk until light and fluffy. Tip into the cream cheese mixture. Quickly whip the cream and tip into the mixture. Fold everything together and pour into the crumb base. Chill overnight.

Simple Ice-cream

3 egg yolks
120 g (just under ½ cup) castor sugar
½ cup alcohol (liqueur, gin or vodka works well)
500 ml cream

Whisk the egg yolks and sugar together in an electric mixer. Whisk in the alcohol. Turn mixer to low and add cream. Add other flavourings, depending on the type of ice-cream you want to create.

Whisk on medium until a soft cream consistency—allow 5 minutes, but do not over-process, otherwise the ice-cream will crumble when frozen.

Pour into a plastic 2 litre ice-cream container and place in the freezer.

For all the ice-cream variations below, make the basic ice-cream as indicated above and add the extras to the mix before freezing.

Maple Walnut
½ cup maple syrup
½ cup chopped walnuts

For this ice-cream reduce the sugar by half, that is, 60 g for the base recipe.

Sour Cherry and Cassis
½ cup Cassis for the alcohol in the basic recipe
1 cup drained and pitted canned cherries (add half while you are beating the mixture and fold in the other half at the end)

Liquorice and Sambuca
½ cup sambuca for the alcohol in the basic recipe
½ cup chopped soft liquorice

To make liquorice soft, just boil it in water until it softens. The liquorice should be just covered with water. Allow to cool before adding to the egg mixture.

Christmas Fruit Compote

This delicious combination of fruit is a perfect instant dessert during the busy summer months. Make up a batch and store it in a large glass jar in the fridge.

1 cup dried apricots, cut in half
1 cup pitted prunes
1 cup large raisins
1 cup sultanas
420 g can sliced peaches
430 g can pineapple pieces
425 g can pitted cherries
½ cup sugar
1 cup brandy
Juice of 2 oranges

Place the apricots, prunes, raisins and sultanas in a saucepan. Drain the juice from the canned fruit into the pan, add the sugar and stir well. Bring to a boil and simmer very gently for 5 minutes. Add the canned peaches, pineapple and cherries. Mix gently, pour in brandy and orange juice and mix well. Pour into a large, clip-lidded jar, ensuring that all the fruit is covered with liquid. More liquor may be added if necessary.

Serve with meringues and whipped cream or crème fraîche.

Simple Ice-cream

Maple and Mustard Barbecued Ham

1 cooked ham
425 g tin pineapple chunks (optional)
½ cup whole grain mustard
¼ cup maple syrup
Whole cloves for garnish

Remove the skin from the ham and make a criss-cross pattern on the ham with a sharp knife. Mix the mustard and maple syrup together and brush all over the top of the ham. Leave a little for basting while the ham is cooking.

Place the cloves in the corners of the criss-cross pattern and scatter the pineapple chunks over the top of the ham.

Place on a large rack over a large oven tray (to collect the cooking juices) and cook indirectly in a covered, preheated barbecue. Cooking indirectly means the heat is on full on the side burners, but directly under the ham the burners are switched off.

If you do not have a covered barbecue you can cook your ham in a 180°C oven for 1½–2 hours.

The pineapple garnish is optional—you can enjoy a delicious hot ham with the mustard and maple syrup alone.

When using the barbecue, allow 2–4 hours and baste with the remaining mustard/maple syrup.

Mango and Lychee Salsa

For a festive occasion—whether it be Christmas or a special celebration—serving a hot glazed ham with a variety of fruit salsas makes great sense. They are fresh, fun and easy to make. Best of all you can prepare them ahead. They also work well with roasted chicken or turkey and any barbecued fare.

425 g tin mango slices
565 g tin whole seedless lychees
2 Tbsp chopped mint
1 Tbsp chopped coriander
½ red onion, finely chopped
A dash of jalapeno sauce or chilli sauce, to taste
Salt and pepper to taste

Drain the canned mango and lychees. Chop into small pieces and place in a bowl.

Add remaining ingredients and mix well.

To make a pawpaw salsa combine half a pawpaw, finely diced, with 2 tablespoons of finely diced red onion, 1 tablespoon finely chopped fresh coriander, salt and pepper and a splash of jalapeno sauce. If you do not have any jalapeno sauce, add just a hint of Tabasco.

Maple and Mustard Barbecued Ham with Fruit Salsas

Easy Yoghurt and Cucumber Dip

Try this superb dip at your next barbecue. Serve it with lamb loins or with char-grilled vegetables (see page 34). It is light and refreshing and is even a happy partner to the humble meat pattie or grilled sausage.

1 cup unsweetened yoghurt
1 telegraph cucumber, grated
2-3 cloves garlic, minced
20 fresh mint leaves, chopped finely
1 Tbsp olive oil
Juice of 1 lemon
¼ tsp cumin
½ tsp ground coriander
Salt and pepper

Squeeze the grated cucumber in a tea towel to remove the excess liquid. Mix in a bowl with all the other ingredients adding salt to taste. Cover and refrigerate till needed. Best eaten on the day it is made.

This is delicious as a sauce to accompany spiced beef in a pita bread.

It makes a superb low-fat accompaniment to salads instead of dressing.

This works well as a cooling agent when eating spicy food.

Lamb Fillet Bacon Wraps

Serves 4
8 lamb fillets
8 tsp whole grain mustard
8 bacon strips
Salad greens
Char-grilled vegetables
1 cup herbed yoghurt dressing*

Take the lamb fillets out of the fridge and have them at room temperature before cooking. Remove any sinew or silver skin from the fillet. Smear each fillet with mustard and wrap the bacon around the fillets. Cook on a very hot plate or grill for approximately 3–4 minutes per side. Leave to rest for a few minutes while you assemble the salad and the pre-cooked char-grilled vegetables.

Cut the lamb fillet on the diagonal and top the salad greens and char-grilled vegetables with the lamb fillets. Drizzle with the herb yoghurt dressing and serve.

*To make the yoghurt dressing just combine 1 cup low-fat natural yoghurt with ¼ cup chopped fresh herbs (parsley, chives, mint, oregano work well), a squeeze of lemon juice and salt and pepper to season.

A delicious addition to a party is to wrap pitted prunes in bacon and grill till golden. These 'devils on horseback' are a universal favourite. For oyster lovers, wrap bacon strips around freshly shucked oysters and grill them till the bacon is golden. Serve these 'angels on horseback' with a supply of toothpicks and mini-napkins.

Warning: they are highly addictive!

Lamb Fillet Bacon Wraps

Feta Toasts

To serve with drinks at your next barbecue. Yum! This recipe is so simple, it's as much a method as it is a detailed recipe.

1 French loaf
½–¾ cup tapenade, pesto, chutney or other full-flavoured spread
200 g feta
Salad greens and fresh herbs (optional)

Slice the French bread and toast on one side. Spread with the pesto or tapenade (olive paste) and top with slices of feta.

Grill for a few minutes until the tops are golden. Note that the cheese will not melt, like on top of a pizza, but keeps its shape well.

Serve immediately.

Chicken Pesto Bacon Wraps

Serves 4
4 chicken breasts, skin on
4 tsp cream cheese
4 tsp sundried tomato or basil pesto
8 rashers bacon

Lift the skin gently from the chicken breast and place the cream cheese and pesto under the skin. Wrap the chicken pesto with 2 rashers of bacon strips, place on a hot grill and cook, turning often, for 15–25 minutes. Alternatively, fan bake in a 200°C oven for 15–20 minutes. Take care with poultry: the juices must run clear.

To make the bacon extra crunchy, place under the grill for a few minutes before serving to give extra colour if desired.

Bacon wrapped around meat during cooking not only provides great flavour but keeps the meat extra moist. I use either middle bacon or bacon strips on these chicken wraps.

A delicious addition to a roast chicken dinner is to serve chunks of banana wrapped in bacon strips and grill till cooked through and golden.

Serve these chicken breasts with char-grilled vegetables and a pesto yoghurt sauce.

Pesto Yoghurt Sauce

½ cup plain yoghurt
2–3 Tbsp pesto
1 Tbsp chopped fresh herbs

Mix all ingredients together, cover and place in the fridge.

Delicious with char-grilled vegetables and as a dipping sauce for a raw vegetable salad or even grilled seafood.

Chicken Pesto Bacon Wraps

Barbecued Salmon Fillet

Barbecued Salmon Fillet

1 side fresh salmon, skin and bones removed
2 large garlic cloves, sliced
Black pepper
Olive oil
Juice of ½ lemon

Dill butter
250 g soft butter
2 tsp lemon juice
1 tsp crushed garlic
2 tsp chopped fresh dill
Cracked pepper

Make the butter first: Mix all the ingredients together in a bowl, place on a piece of foil and roll into a sausage shape. Chill for about 1–2 hours until firm. Unroll and slice into 1.25 cm thick rounds and place in cold water until needed.

To prepare the salmon: Stud the sliced garlic randomly all over the fillet. Grind black pepper on top and place in 2 large sheets of tin foil that have been oiled. Drizzle a little more olive oil over with the lemon juice. Fold up the foil into a parcel. Place on a baking tray in a preheated low barbecue for approximately 10–15 minutes or until pale pink and still medium rare.

Remove from heat. Open parcel and top with dill butter. Serve.

Slicing the butter in advance and keeping the slices in cold water is a great way to ease up when serving a crowd. If you are simply cooking salmon or any other fish on the barbecue and need to enhance it a little, pop a thin slice of dill butter on the fish just prior to serving. As the butter melts, the dill will cover the fish—superb flavours guaranteed.

Italian Butter

2 cloves garlic, crushed
2 tomatoes, peeled, seeded and finely chopped
¼ cup fresh basil, finely minced
1 Tbsp finely chopped oregano
½ tsp salt
Freshly ground black pepper
125 g softened butter

Blend the garlic, tomatoes, basil, oregano, salt and pepper with the butter. Shape into a roll and wrap in foil. Place in fridge.

Delicious to smear under chicken skin before grilling or perhaps a small knob to top a grilled steak.

Anchovy Butter

3 anchovy fillets, minced
1 spring onion, finely chopped
1 Tbsp lemon juice
Freshly ground black pepper
1–2 Tbsp freshly chopped parsley
125 g butter, softened

Blend all the ingredients together with the butter. Shape and wrap in foil and place in fridge.

Anchovies are a delicious addition to lamb. You could try smearing a little anchovy butter over lamb chops prior to grilling or perhaps a light smear of this butter on a roast leg of lamb before baking in the oven.

Grilled Blue Cheese Mushrooms

This simple treatment of mushrooms really celebrates the full flavour of good blue cheese.

Serves 6

6 large, flat mushrooms
1–2 tsp butter
6 cloves garlic, finely minced
200 g wedges blue vein cheese, crumbled
3 Tbsp toasted pine nuts
Grilled bacon and a favourite balsamic dressing for garnish

Place the mushrooms underside down in a pan with the garlic and the butter. Cook slowly, adjusting the heat as necessary, spooning any juices (which will be full of garlic flavour) over the mushrooms. Allow 5 minutes of gentle cooking.

Cut each 100 g wedge of cheese into 3 slices so you will have 6 generous slices. Cut these into 2 (a total of 12 pieces).

Place a slice of blue cheese on top of each mushroom and allow to melt. Covering the pan with a lid will help at this stage, or you could place under the grill for a minute.

When the cheese is melted and bubbling, top with grilled bacon and toasted pine nuts if desired, drizzle a little balsamic dressing over and serve immediately.

Potato and Cheese Bake

If you are looking for a filling, delicious and inexpensive family vegetable suggestion then why not combine the popular potato with a lower-fat cheese. Edam is so easy to eat and that block in the fridge is extremely versatile—you will love this recipe!

Serves 6-8

4 medium potatoes
1 bunch chives or ½ green capsicum, finely chopped
1 onion, finely chopped
1 cup milk
3 large eggs
1 tsp salt
Freshly ground black pepper
1 cup edam cheese, grated
2 Tbsp soft butter

Grate the potatoes and place in a large bowl with the chives or capsicum and onion. Put the milk, eggs, salt and pepper, cheese and butter in a food processor or blender. Process, then mix well with the vegetables. If you do not have a food processor you can mix all the ingredients together in the large bowl.

Spray a large casserole lightly with oil, add vegetable mixture and bake for 1½ hours at 180°C. Garnish with bacon 30 minutes before end of cooking time.

This is a great recipe for family dinners and entertaining. It's a very smart dish to accompany a platter of barbecued delights (from seafood to chicken to sausages) as well as a stunning dinner suggestion to serve with a simple roasted chicken.

Potato and Cheese Bake; Grilled Blue Cheese Mushrooms

Spinach, Seafood and Feta Salad

Try this at your next barbecue. Just char-grill your favourite seafood quickly—I have used calamari—and combine with fresh spinach, chunks of feta, freshly cooked bacon and slices of red onion. Toss through some pine nuts and top with this simple blue cheese dressing.

Serves 4

500 g spinach
4–5 cups cooked calamari
200 g feta cheese, diced
½ red onion, thinly sliced
200 g shoulder bacon
½ cup toasted pine nuts

Simple Blue Cheese Dressing
1 cup mayonnaise
100 g blue vein cheese
¼ cup buttermilk

Process in a food processor until smooth.

To assemble the salad: Wash and dry the spinach. Break manageable pieces into a large salad bowl. Add the calamari, cheese, and sprinkle through the red onion slices. Remove the rind from the bacon and grill. Cut into chunks and place on top of the salad. Drizzle with salad dressing. Top with pine nuts. Serve.

If pine nuts are too expensive, just omit from the recipe or leave them for a special occasion.

Invest in a mini food processor or kitchen whiz to help with making great dressings.

Creamy Herb Dressing

Try this dressing as well with the spinach seafood and feta salad.

1½ cups sour cream
1 cup mayonnaise
1¼ cups buttermilk
¼ cup white vinegar
2 Tbsp honey
1 Tbsp Dijon mustard
1 Tbsp chopped garlic
2 Tbsp chopped parsley
2 Tbsp chopped tarragon
2 Tbsp chopped chives
2 Tbsp chopped fresh dill

In a large bowl combine all the ingredients. Stir until well blended. Store the dressing, covered, for at least 4 hours before serving. Makes approximately 4 cups.

This recipe can be halved.

Spinach, Seafood and Feta Salad

Mussel, Prawn and Pasta Salad

You can either divide this onto 4 plates all ready for serving or impress friends and family with your gourmet cooking by placing it all in a large bowl or platter. It looks terribly chic and, best of all, tastes wonderful. Make sure the seafood is super-fresh!

Serves 4

2 cups uncooked pasta shells
500 g mesclun mix or salad greens
2 cups cooked prawns
2 cups cooked mussels, shells removed
½ cup sliced sundried tomatoes
1 cup crème fraîche
Salt and pepper
2 spring onions, finely sliced

Cook the pasta in salted, boiling water until al dente. Divide the mesclun or salad greens between 4 plates, then do the same with the prawns, mussels and pasta.

Mix the sundried tomatoes with the crème fraîche, season well and place spoonfuls lightly on each plate on or near the pasta. Finish with slices of spring onions.

Serve.

Feta Wraps with a Herbed Yoghurt Sauce

Feta adds a zing of flavour to this salad wrap. Use whatever fillings you desire in this 'wrap food to go' suggestion. When we were testing these wraps at home they were so tempting that we unfortunately sampled one straight away. All work stopped and all the wraps were consumed—these are sensational!

Serves 4

4 small pita breads
Salad greens
1 double chicken breast, roasted and skin removed
⅔ cup sliced and char-grilled peppers
½ red onion, finely sliced
100 g feta, thinly sliced

Yoghurt Herb Dressing
1 cup natural yoghurt
2 tsp mint jelly
¼ telegraph cucumber, peeled and finely diced
2 tsp Thai sweet chilli sauce

Make the dressing by combining all ingredients and reserve.

Heat the pita breads in the microwave—30 seconds for 2 warms them perfectly.

Spoon a little dressing onto the bread, top with salad greens and a quarter of the chicken, char-grilled peppers, red onion and feta. Spoon a little more dressing onto the wrap and roll up.

Serve with a napkin.

Very filling and great flavours!

We used Galaxy feta in these wraps.

Mussel, Prawn and Pasta Salad

Easy Mushroom and Bacon Pasta

This is so super-simple you will be thrilled. Serve in a large bowl with salad and perhaps some bread to help mop up all the great sauce.

1 onion, chopped
3 cloves garlic, minced
2–3 Tbsp olive oil
1–2 tsp dried thyme or 3–4 tsp fresh thyme
5 rashers (200 g) lean bacon, chopped and rind removed
6–7 cups (approximately 600 g) chopped mushrooms
1 cup (250 g) crème fraîche
Pepper to season
Dash of jalapeno sauce (optional)
400 g fresh egg tagliatelle

Place a large pot of salted water on to boil for the pasta. In a large frypan or pot sauté the onion and garlic in the olive oil for 5 minutes on a low heat. Add the thyme and cook for a further 1–2 minutes. Add the bacon and stir and sauté for another few minutes. Now add the chopped mushrooms and cook until the mushrooms have softened.

Cook the pasta according to the instructions on the packet. Drain.

Add the crème fraîche to the mushrooms and, when completely integrated, season the sauce and add the cooked pasta.

Divine Macaroni Cheese

To celebrate the launch of Mainland's new smoked cheese—a natural cheese that has been smoked, not processed—I created this superb re-make of a classic family favourite. The smoked flavour pervades the dish, but does not dominate.

½ onion
5 whole cloves
2 bay leaves
750 ml milk
500 g packet macaroni
75 g butter
75 g (approximately ½ cup) flour
250 g smoked cheese, grated
125 g edam cheese, grated
100 g parmesan cheese, grated
½ tsp ground nutmeg
Salt and pepper to taste
1½ cups fresh breadcrumbs
4 rashers bacon, rindless and chopped

Stud the peeled half onion with the cloves and place in a pot with the bay leaves and the milk. Heat the milk till it simmers, place the lid on the pot and remove from the heat and allow the flavours to infuse for 10 minutes.

Cook the pasta according to the instructions on the packet. Drain and reserve.

Drain the milk into a jug.

While the milk is still warm, heat the butter in a large pot, When completely melted add the flour and stir over a low heat until the mixture forms a smooth paste. Cook the mixture, stirring constantly, for another minute. Add the warm milk a little at a time, whisking well after each addition. Allow the mixture to thicken up after each addition of milk, before adding more.

Continue adding all the milk and stir and simmer for 10 minutes on a gentle heat. The stirring prevents lumps from forming.

Preheat the oven to 180°C. Combine the cheeses and add three-quarters to the sauce. Combine the remaining quarter with the fresh breadcrumbs and reserve for the topping.

Combine the macaroni and cheese sauce and pour into a large gratin dish. Scatter the topping over the pasta.

Top with the chopped bacon and bake at 180°C for 30–40 minutes.

Divine Macaroni Cheese

Mini Meat Loaf with Blue Cheese and Bacon

Mini Meat Loaf with Blue Cheese and Bacon

Makes 6

60 g spicy bacon, diced
½ onion, diced
Olive oil
2 white mushrooms, chopped
500 g minced beef
1 egg
⅛ cup or 30 ml cream
125 g gruyère cheese, grated
¼ cup cornflakes
6 Tbsp blue cheese
6 rashers middle bacon

Preheat the oven to 180°C fan bake.

In a pan, sauté the bacon and onion in a little olive oil. Add the sliced mushrooms.

In a separate bowl, mix the beef, egg and cream. Add the onion mix to the beef with the gruyère cheese and the cornflakes.

Divide the mixture into 6 even portions and place 1 tablespoon of blue cheese into each. Form into rectangular logs and wrap bacon around.

Bake for approximately 30 minutes.

Serve with creamy mashed potatoes and a salad, with Thai sweet chilli sauce as an accompaniment if desired.

Oven Roasted Vegetables

This is simply a means of making crunchy, great-tasting vegetables rather than a specific recipe. It was created one night when cooking in a hurry for a hungry family. You will be delighted with the results—these vegetables are super crispy!

Serves 4–6

4–6 potatoes, peeled and cut into 1.25 cm slices
4–6 kumara, peeled and cut into 1.25 cm slices
Olive oil
Sea salt
Freshly ground pepper
4 cloves garlic, unpeeled
2–4 sprigs fresh rosemary

Preheat the oven to 200°C.

Place the potatoes and kumara in a large microwave-proof bowl. Do not add any liquid. Cover with plastic wrap and microwave on high for 10 minutes. Place in a large roasting pan and drizzle with the olive oil. Lightly scatter the sea salt over the top together with a good grinding of black pepper. Place the garlic in the tray, unpeeled. Run your hand down the fresh rosemary to break the leaves from the stem over the roasting tray.

Bake at 200°C for 20 minutes or until the desired degree of golden colour is obtained.

Family Dinners   Annabelle Cooks

Martha's Vineyard Casserole

This recipe makes a large casserole—perfect for entertaining. A friend made it for me one summer at Martha's Vineyard on the eastern shores of the US and ever since it has been a firm family favourite. Serve it with a mixed green salad.

Serves 8–12
375 g pasta shells
250 g sour cream
125 g cream cheese
A small bunch spring onions, chopped
Parsley, chopped
Salt and pepper
6–8 cups meat sauce*
1 cup grated aged cheddar cheese

Cook the pasta according to the instructions on the packet. Drain and add the sour cream and cream cheese to the hot pasta. Leave for a few minutes then stir through gently. Add the spring onions and parsley. Season with salt and pepper.

In a large greased casserole dish place a layer of pasta, top with meat sauce and then repeat. Top with grated cheese.

Bake at 180°C for 40 minutes.

*For the meat sauce cook 700 g mince with 3 cloves garlic, 1 chopped onion and herbs (basil and oregano) to taste, then add 3 cups chopped mushrooms, a 400 g tin of tomatoes and a good slosh of red wine! Cook slowly for 20–30 minutes. If it gets too dry add a little more wine, water or beef stock, but it should not be too sloppy. You can just cook 700 g mince with a jar of commercial tomato pasta sauce if preferred.

This casserole is delicious made the day before as the flavours are enhanced with resting. Allow 60 minutes to reheat from fridge temperature.

Smoked Chicken and Avocado Pasta

The crème fraîche provides the delicious sauce to accompany the smoked chicken and avocado. As these ingredients enjoy gentle preparation, the quick cooking time associated with crème fraîche is ideal. This instant pasta sauce couldn't be easier and it's so divine!

Serves 4–6
250 g penne pasta
Olive oil to coat the pasta
Chopped parsley to coat the pasta
1 double breast smoked chicken
1 medium onion, chopped
1 knob butter
250 g crème fraîche
½ cup chicken stock or water or white wine
1 avocado, sliced
Salt and pepper to season
½ cup toasted pine nuts
Crispy bacon and freshly sliced parmesan to garnish

Cook the pasta according to the instructions on the packet. Toss in a little oil and freshly chopped parsley. Divide and slice the smoked chicken into manageable pieces.

In a large frying pan, melt the butter completely, add the chopped onion and gently sweat till translucent but not brown.

Add the crème fraîche and chicken stock and heat through gently. Add the diced smoked chicken and heat through until the chicken is hot. Add the avocado, season with salt and pepper and heat through again, taking care not to over-mix the sauce.

Serve over the hot pasta and top with grilled bacon and slices of parmesan for garnish.

For a great taste sensation try a splash of jalapeno sauce with this recipe.

Smoked Chicken and Avocado Pasta

Yorkshire Puddings with Frankfurters

Remember the classic toad-in-the-hole where your mother or grandmother would whip up a roasting pan of Yorkshire pud with sausages for an easy supper? The key was to eat this delicious offering as soon as it emerged from the oven. In large families, the number of sausage 'bits' you received on your plate often indicated your popularity with the cook. This is an easy, inexpensive, filling dinner but also a sensational breakfast treat with warmed maple syrup.

Serves 4 (makes 12 muffin-sized Yorkshire puds)

6 Tbsp plain flour
1 tsp salt
2 eggs
1¾ cups milk
6 tsp lard
6 frankfurters, halved

Whisk the flour, salt, eggs and milk until bubbles form on top. Leave for half an hour.

Preheat the oven to 200°C fan bake. Divide up the lard with the frankfurters among the 12 greased muffin pans. Place in the oven for 10 minutes.

Remove from the oven, whisk the pudding mix again, then pour on top of the frankfurters.

Bake for 20 minutes or until batter has risen and is golden. Serve immediately.

Easy Lemon Chicken

Serves 4

4 single chicken breasts
2 large potatoes, diced
Salt and pepper
½ cup vegetable oil
2 Tbsp lemon juice
2 tsp minced garlic
1½ tsp Italian seasoning

Preheat oven to 180°C. Arrange chicken in a single layer in a shallow pan. Arrange potatoes in the same pan. Sprinkle lightly with salt and pepper. Combine vegetable oil, lemon juice, garlic and seasoning together and brush onto chicken and potatoes. Bake at 180°C for 50–55 minutes or until chicken is done and potatoes are tender when tested with a fork.

Serve with a salad and steamed green beans.

You could serve this family favourite with herbed bread. Make your favourite garlic butter—crush garlic, mix with softened butter and add some finely chopped fresh green herbs like parsley, basil or oregano. Smear over the bread slices, wrap in tin foil and cook until warmed through and the butter has melted completely. For other butter suggestions see page 49.

Yorkshire Puddings with Frankfurters

Mussel and Bacon Pasta

Serves 4

250 g fettucine pasta
200 g shoulder bacon, chopped
1 onion, chopped
3 cloves garlic
1 tsp minced fresh ginger
250 g crème fraîche
500 g mussels, chopped
Salt and pepper to taste
2–3 tsp Thai sweet chilli sauce
2–3 Tbsp chopped fresh parsley

While the pasta is cooking as per the instructions on the packet, make the sauce. Place the bacon, onion, garlic and ginger in a large, hot pan. When the bacon has cooked and the onion is soft add the crème fraîche and mussels and season with salt, pepper and chilli sauce. Add the chopped parsley and the hot pasta.

Serve with a tossed salad.

The simplicity and versatility of crème fraîche is a joy to the busy home cook. As soon as the crème fraîche is added, you have your sauce. It has the ability to withstand high temperatures without separating and there is no need for reducing your sauce—it's ready to go!

I use mussels in brine from the supermarket—just drain the mussels and chop them up! The extra acidity from the brine works well in this recipe.

Alison's Pasta Salami Bake

A busy mum in Wellington, Alison Dyer, gave me this recipe and said her children loved any excuse to eat salami. She found that matching salami with tomatoes, pasta and cheese made her a very popular cook in her household.

375 g pasta spirals or penne pasta
400 g tin seasoned Italian tomatoes
½ an Italian salami, cut into chunks
3–4 spring onions, chopped
½ cup chopped parsley
1½ cups diced edam cheese
Salt and pepper to taste
½ cup grated parmesan cheese for topping

Cook the pasta according to the instructions on the packet and drain in a colander.

Tip drained pasta into a greased casserole dish and add the tomatoes, salami chunks, spring onions, chopped parsley and edam cheese and season with salt and pepper.

Top with grated parmesan cheese and bake at 200°C for 20–30 minutes.

Serve with a mixed green salad.

Mussel and Bacon Pasta

Basic Pizza Dough

Once you have tried this recipe you will be hooked—there will never be enough time to eat all the pizzas you will make. It is so simple and so delicious.

1 tsp active dry yeast
⅔ cup warm water
2 cups plain flour
1 tsp salt
1 tsp oregano
1 tsp crushed garlic
Olive oil

Dissolve the yeast in warm water. Leave for 5 minutes. Stir until the yeast dissolves. Add to the flour, salt, oregano and garlic in a large bowl. Mix until combined thoroughly. Form into a large ball and place in a bowl that has been lightly oiled. Turn the dough to the top so the oiled side is exposed.

Cover and place in a warm, draught-free area for 2 hours or until doubled in size. This mix can be left overnight.

After this resting period you can push the dough down and knead it gently on a lightly floured surface. Divide the dough in half and stretch and roll out each piece to about 20 cm circumference. Do not roll the dough too thinly. Place in pizza trays (sprayed with olive oil) or straight onto an oven tray (sprayed with olive oil).

Suggested toppings

Salmon and Crème Fraîche Pizza

For 1 pizza:
½ cup crème fraîche
¼ red onion, finely sliced
1 cup smoked or fresh salmon
Cracked pepper
Drained capers (optional)

Preheat the oven to 180°C fan bake. Spread two-thirds of the crème fraîche onto the pizza base. Cover the pizza almost to the sides. Place half of the red onion over the crème fraîche, then scatter the salmon over, then the remaining red onion slices and seasoning. Dollop the remaining crème fraîche onto the pizza and scatter the drained capers if desired.

Bake at 180°C for approximately 20 minutes. Check to ensure the pizza is cooked by lifting the base up gently with a fish slice. When the base is an even, golden colour, remove from the oven.

Serve with a tossed salad.

Camembert and Salami Pizza

For this recipe follow the same steps as above, but instead of the crème fraîche and salmon use the following ingredients.

For 1 pizza:
⅓ cup of your favourite tomato-based chutney
100 g sliced brie or camembert
⅔ cup diced or sliced salami
You will also need the sliced red onion and cracked black pepper from above

Smear the pizza base with the chutney and scatter the remaining ingredients over the top. Bake as above.

Salmon and Crème Fraîche Pizza

Nectarine Buttermilk Tart

Nectarine Buttermilk Tart

A perfect celebration of stone fruits!

Serves 6–8

400 g packet sweet short pastry
2 egg yolks
1 egg
⅓ cup brown sugar, firmly packed
½ tsp vanilla
1 Tbsp plain flour
¾ tsp cinnamon
¼ tsp ground nutmeg
¾ cup buttermilk
½ cup cream
4 nectarines (each cut into 6 pieces)

Preheat oven to 160°C. Roll out pastry and line a 23 cm spring-form tin or pie plate. Mix egg yolks, egg, brown sugar and vanilla. Add flour, cinnamon and nutmeg. In a saucepan, warm the buttermilk and cream. Place to one side to cool. Whisk the warm buttermilk/cream into the egg mixture.

Place sliced nectarines in the pastry case and pour egg mix over the nectarines. Bake for 45–55 minutes or until set.

Serve with whipped cream, dusted with nutmeg.

Best eaten the day it is made and warm, not hot. You can make it ahead, but do not place in the fridge—if served too cold all the flavour is lost.

Lemon Buttermilk Cake

A slice of this cake, without icing, is a memorable base for fresh berries and whipped cream. If you ice the cake, serve it up with copious cups of tea for friends and family.

170 g butter, at room temperature
1½ cups sugar
2 Tbsp grated lemon peel
3 large eggs
¼ cup fresh lemon juice
3 cups flour
1 tsp baking soda
¼ tsp salt
1½ cups buttermilk

Preheat the oven to 180°C. Butter and flour a 24 cm cake tin. Cream the butter and sugar with the lemon peel. Add eggs one at a time, beating well after each addition. Beat in lemon juice. Sift the flour, baking soda and salt into a medium bowl. Stir dry ingredients into butter mixture alternately with the buttermilk, beginning and ending with dry ingredients. Bake at 180°C for 40–50 minutes or until a skewer comes cleanly from the cake.

Ice with lemon and passionfruit cream cheese icing or ice with a plain lemon icing. We also drizzled warm commercial passionfruit syrup over the cake as soon as it came out of the oven.

Gingered Pear Sour Cream Pie

Pears and ginger work very well together. Add a little sour cream and you create a full flavour with a creamy, luscious backdrop. Use fresh pears for this recipe and serve warm or at room temperature, not hot.

23 cm pie dish lined with sweet shortcrust pastry

Topping
¼ cup flour
50 g butter, diced
3 Tbsp brown sugar
1 tsp ginger
Pinch of salt
1 cup finely chopped walnuts

Filling
¾ cup sour cream
2 large eggs, beaten lightly
½ cup brown sugar
2 Tbsp flour
2 tsp ground ginger
2 tsp lemon juice
500 g pears, peeled, cored and sliced thinly
Crème fraîche or cream for decoration

Preheat the oven to 220°C. Place pie weights, such as rice, on the pie shell, cover with foil and bake blind for 10–15 minutes.

Make the streusel topping: In a bowl blend the first measure of flour, butter, brown sugar, ginger and salt until the mixture resembles coarse meal. You could do this stage in a food processor if desired.

Add the chopped walnuts and toss through well.

Prepare the filling: In a food processor or a large bowl combine the sour cream, eggs, brown sugar, flour, ginger and lemon juice until the mixture is smooth.

Gently stir in the thinly sliced pears. Coat them with the mixture and transfer the filling to the pastry shell.

Sprinkle the streusel topping evenly over the filling and bake at 220°C for 15 minutes, then reduce heat to 180°C and bake for 30 minutes more till golden and the filling is set.

If you want to get a little fancy, you could add some very finely diced ginger in syrup to some softened vanilla ice-cream. Refreeze and serve a scoop with this pie. Ginger in syrup is often found in the bulk bin section of the supermarket.

Baked Orange Cheesecake

Smooth, luxurious and rich, this will feed a crowd. It's so popular, seconds may be demanded so serve small slices!

400 g sweet short pastry
600 g cream cheese
225 g or approx ¾ cup castor sugar
1½ Tbsp plain flour
Juice from 2 oranges
1 Tbsp orange zest
2 eggs and 1 yolk

Preheat the oven to fan bake 160°C. Line a greased 20 cm spring-form tin with rolled-out pastry.

In a mixer, blend the cream cheese and castor sugar until lump free. Add flour, juice, zest, eggs and yolk.

Spoon into the prepared tin lined with pastry and bake on the middle shelf for approximately 40 minutes or until firm in the centre.

Delicious served with softly whipped cream or crème fraîche with a little orange curd or orange juice mixed together and a dusting of orange zest.

Do not use the spreadable cream cheese for this recipe—the traditional cream cheese is best for this cheesecake.

Baked Orange Cheesecake

Almond Apricot Chews

These are the most deliciously simple biscuits to make and are a great means of using up a leftover egg white. For example, if you were making the citrus biscuits on page 76 and you had a leftover egg white, whip these up and serve them with the citrus biscuits instead of dessert at the end of a meal.

250 g ground almonds
80 g or ½ cup chopped dates
80 g (⅓ cup) sugar
1 tsp orange rind
60 ml maple syrup
80 g (½ cup) chopped dried apricots
1 egg white
50 g (⅔ cup) desiccated coconut

Preheat the oven to 180°C. Grease an oven tray. Place all the ingredients except the coconut in a food processor. Process until a chunky paste. Divide into 24 balls. Roll in coconut and press down slightly with a fork. Bake at 180°C for 10–15 minutes.

They should be light brown and slightly chewy in the centre.

Store in an airtight container.

Great for morning coffee. Try them—they are so easy!

Sour Cream Chocolate Cake

Everyone loves a chocolate cake and this one is simple and a real crowd-pleaser. It makes a large cake—I used a 26 cm spring-form pan. Split in half and ice the middle, top and sides with chocolate icing. Serve a slice with a scoop of vanilla ice-cream.

250 g softened butter
2 cups sugar
4 large eggs
250 g sour cream
2½ cups flour
½ cup cocoa
2 tsp baking soda
½ tsp salt
1 cup dark chocolate bits

Preheat the oven to 180°C or 160°C fan bake.

Lightly cream the butter and sugar. Beat in the eggs and sour cream. Add the dry ingredients and the chocolate bits. Place in a greased and floured 26 cm spring-form tin. Bake for 60–80 minutes. Check with a skewer after 60 minutes.

You can spray the tin with oil spray, rather than grease and flour it, and the results are fine.

My preference with cakes is not to use fan bake. In my kitchen fan bake is used for muffins and biscuits and when the oven is full of cooking.

Sour Cream Chocolate Cake

Chateau Yering Tea Cakes

Sitting proudly in Australia's Yarra Valley in Victoria this luxurious accommodation serves up these delicious warm tea cakes on their local cheese platters. They make up a large batch in advance and, when cool, wrap individually in plastic wrap to freeze. They then defrost them as needed (still in the wrap) in the microwave for a few seconds.

Makes 12 muffins
100 g (about ½ cup) demerara sugar
140 ml strong hot tea
400 g (2½ cups) sultanas
1 beaten egg
1 Tbsp milk
225 g (just under 2 cups) self-raising flour

Preheat the oven to 170°C regular bake, not fan bake.

Dissolve sugar in hot tea and add to the sultanas. When cool, add the egg, milk and self-raising flour.

Grease a 12-muffin tray and divide the mixture evenly into the pans.

Bake at 170°C for 20 minutes.

Grilled Summer Fruit with Crème Fraîche

Several years ago while visiting Hawke's Bay for the Wine and Food festival I had the most superb dinner at the Brookfields Winery with winemaker Peter Robertson and chef Vicki Bruhns-Bolderson. It was a sultry February evening and the dessert captured the season, the celebration and the relaxed tone of the evening perfectly.

Serves 4
8 ripe nectarines
8 ripe apricots
½ cup orange juice or brandy
4 Tbsp sugar

Citrus Passionfruit Cream
250 g (1 cup) crème fraîche
3 Tbsp lemon curd or fresh orange juice
4 fresh passionfruit or 3 Tbsp passionfruit pulp
Icing sugar for dusting

Cut the fruit in half and remove the stones. Place in a large roasting tray with the cut side up. Drizzle with brandy or orange juice. Sprinkle with the sugar. Grill on high until the sugar starts to caramelise, about 10 minutes.

While the fruit is grilling, combine the crème fraîche with the lemon curd or orange juice and passionfruit pulp. Place in a bowl or side dish to accompany the platter of warm grilled fruits.

You can use orange juice instead of brandy if you prefer. For great texture, serve with biscotti or home-made cookies.

The bonus here is that you can prepare the cream as the fruit is grilling. A dessert has never been so easy.

You can also serve natural yoghurt with the lemon curd and passionfruit for a lower-fat option.

Grilled Summer Fruit with Crème Fraîche

Pumpkin Maple Sour Cream Pie

When I lived in the United States, pumpkin pie and pumpkin bread were always associated with Thanksgiving. Friends and neighbours would arrive on your doorstep towards the end of November with cellophane-wrapped baked pumpkin goodies to mark the season. This pie will bring much delight to your friends and family—it's irresistible. The sour cream lightens the pumpkin flavour.

375 g cream cheese, softened
¾ cup sugar
1 tsp cinnamon
¼ cup maple syrup
1 tsp vanilla
3 eggs
½ cup sour cream
2 cups mashed cooked pumpkin
¾ cup plain flour
400 g sweet short pastry

Preheat the oven to 160°C fan bake or 180°C normal bake. Make sure the oven rack is set at the bottom of the oven.

Put cream cheese, sugar and cinnamon in a large bowl and combine together with an electric mixer. Add maple syrup, vanilla, eggs, sour cream, pumpkin and flour.

Blend until just combined, no more.

Roll out pastry and place in a greased 24 cm flan tin. Pour in the pumpkin mixture.

Bake until firm in the centre. Check after 35–40 minutes.

Serve warm, not hot, with whipped cream topped with a dusting of cinnamon or nutmeg.

Citrus Biscuits

These simple biscuits will keep well in the tin for a week. They make a great present. Just find a suitable container, fill with the biscuits and top it off with a yellow ribbon.

Makes about 32 biscuits
60 g butter
1 tsp vanilla essence
¼ cup castor sugar
1 egg yolk
1 tsp very finely minced orange rind
1 cup self-raising flour
¼ tsp baking soda
2 Tbsp sour cream

Citrus Icing
1 cup icing sugar
2 tsp grated orange rind
2 Tbsp orange juice
1 Tbsp lemon juice

Lightly grease the oven trays and preheat the oven to 180°C.

Cream the butter, essence, sugar, egg yolk and orange rind in a small bowl with the electric mixer until just combined.

Stir in the sifted dry ingredients and sour cream in 2 batches. Roll rounded teaspoons of mixture into balls. Place onto prepared trays. Press tops lightly with a fork.

Bake at 180°C for about 10 minutes or until lightly browned. Leave on the trays for 5 minutes before lifting onto wire racks to cool.

Ice the biscuits when cool and return to the wire racks to set.

To make the icing: Combine the sifted icing sugar, rind and strained juices in a small bowl. Stir and heat in microwave for 20 seconds at a time until desired consistency.

These biscuits are delicious served with softened vanilla ice-cream that has had lemon curd or a splash of Lemoncello lemon liqueur added to it and refrozen. If that sounds like too much work, serve the biscuits for dessert with parfait glasses of the best vanilla ice-cream with one nip of Lemoncello poured over it. Lemoncello (also known as Limoncello) is available in specialty food stores and is an Italian lemon liqueur. It is delicious served chilled at the conclusion of a dinner party.

Pumpkin Maple Sour Cream Pie

Sundried Tomato and Feta Spread (foreground); Blue Cheese Dressing (background)

Sundried Tomato and Feta Spread

Feta and sundried tomato make happy partners. Like other delights from the Mediterranean—such as olives and fresh herbs—mixing together with cream cheese and sour cream will quickly create a delicious spread.

6–8 sundried tomatoes
150 g sour cream
2 tsp chopped garlic chives
3 tsp chopped fresh basil
1 Tbsp mayonnaise
100 g crumbled feta cheese
100 g cream cheese
Freshly ground black pepper

In a bowl, mix together all the ingredients except the sundried tomatoes.

Cut the sundried tomatoes into strips and stir through the mixture. Cover and refrigerate until serving. Serve as a generous spread with a basket of bread.

John's Kumara and Rosemary Spread

This is a delightful mix of savoury kumara and bacon with a rich, creamy partnership—enjoy!

4 small-sized kumaras, peeled and cooked
1 Tbsp butter
Pinch salt
Freshly ground black pepper
4 rashers bacon, grilled and finely chopped
150 g light sour cream
2 tsp chopped fresh garlic chives
1 tsp curry powder
2 Tbsp mayonnaise
4 tsp chopped fresh rosemary
100 g light cream cheese

Mash the cooked kumara with butter and seasoning. In another bowl mix the sour cream, chives, curry powder, mayonnaise, rosemary and cream cheese.

Add mashed kumara and bacon to the sour cream mix. Chill.

Serve with toasted sundried tomato or herb bread.

Blue Cheese Dressing

A delicious addition to a spinach and bacon salad. I usually add chunks of blue vein cheese to the salad as well—being a firm believer that you can never have enough of a good thing!

100 g creamy blue or blue vein cheese
250 ml cream
1 Tbsp cognac
Pinch of cayenne pepper
2 Tbsp white wine vinegar

Place all the ingredients in a food processor or blender and whirl till smooth. Let stand for 10 minutes.

Simple Buttermilk Dressing

⅓ cup mayonnaise
⅓ cup buttermilk
¾ tsp finely grated lemon peel
1 tsp fresh lemon juice
¼ tsp salt
1–2 tsp horseradish

Combine all the ingredients.

See also the recipe for Creamy Herb Dressing on page 52.

Index — Annabelle Cooks

Alison's Pasta Salami Bake 64
Almond Apricot Chews 72
Anchovy Butter 49
Antipasto 34
Apricot Buttermilk Muffins 14

Bacon and Mushroom Pasta 56
Bacon and Mussel Pasta 64
Bacon, Chicken, Brie Salad 30
Bacon, Chicken Pesto Wraps 46
Bacon, Lamb Fillet Wraps 44
Bake, Pasta, Salami 64
Bake, Potato and Cheese 50
Baked Orange Cheesecake 70
Banana-Nut Loaf 19
Barbecued Salmon Fillet 49
Basic Pizza Dough 66
Biscuits, Citrus 76
Blue Cheese and Parsnip Soup 24
Blue Cheese Dressing 79
Blue Cheese Mushrooms, Grilled 50
Blue Cheese Vegetable and
    Bacon Tarts 32
Blueberry Cheesecake Brownies 20
Bread, Turkish 34
Brownies, Blueberry Cheesecake 20
Butter, Anchovy 49
Butter, Italian 49
Buttermilk, Fruit-filled Scones 19
Buttermilk, Lemon Cake 69

Cake, Delicious Orange Sour Cream 22
Cake, Lemon Buttermilk 69
Cake, Sour Cream Chocolate 72
Camembert and Salami Pizza 66
Camembert Omelette 12
Casserole, Martha's Vineyard 60
Char-grilled Vegetables 34
Chateau Yering Tea Cakes 74
Cheese and Potato Bake 50
Cheesecake, Baked Orange 70
Cheesecake, Blueberry Brownies 20
Cheesecake, Fuss-free Lemon 39
Chicken Parmesan 36
Chicken Pesto Bacon Wraps 46
Chicken, Brie and Bacon Salad 30
Chicken, Easy Lemon 62
Chilled Cucumber, Avocado
    and Yoghurt Soup 26
Chocolate and Coconut Sour
    Cream Loaf 20
Christmas Fruit Compote 40
Citrus Biscuits 76
Coconut and Chocolate Sour
    Cream Loaf 20
Compote, Christmas Fruit 40
Courgette Cheese Pie 29
Creamy Herb Dressing 52
Crème Fraîche with Grilled
    Summer Fruit 74
Crêpes, Double Cream Camembert and
    Chicken 32
Crisp Potato Cake served with
    Bacon and Eggs 14

Delicious Orange Sour Cream Cake 22
Delicious Flan Pastry 36
Dip, Easy Yoghurt and Cucumber 44
Divine Macaroni Cheese 56
Double Cream Camembert and
    Chicken Crêpes 32
Dressing, Blue Cheese 79
Dressing, Creamy Herb 52
Dressing, Simple Buttermilk 79

Easy Bran Muffins 16
Easy Lemon Chicken 62
Easy Mushroom and Bacon Pasta 56
Easy Tuna Flan 36
Easy Yoghurt and Cucumber Dip 44

Feta Toasts 46
Feta Wraps with a Herbed
    Yoghurt Sauce 54
Flan, Easy Tuna 36
Fondue, Leek 26
Fruit and Banana Smoothie 10
Fruit Salad Smoothie 10
Fruit-filled Buttermilk Scones 19
Fuss-free Lemon Cheesecake 39

Gingered Pear Sour Cream Pie 70
Grilled Blue Cheese Mushrooms 50
Grilled Summer Fruit with
    Crème Fraîche 74

Ham, Maple and Mustard Barbecued 42

Ice-cream, Simple 40
Impossible-to-Fail Quiche 29
Italian Butter 49

John's Fruit and Nut Porridge 12
John's Kumara and Rosemary Spread 79

Lamb Fillet Bacon Wraps 44
Leek Fondue 26
Lemon Buttermilk Cake 69
Loaf, Banana-Nut 19
Loaf, Chocolate and Coconut
    Sour Cream 20

Macaroni Cheese 56
Mango and Lychee Salsa 42
Maple and Mustard Barbecued Ham 42
Maple Syrup Glazed Pears 39
Martha's Vineyard Casserole 60
Mash, Root Vegetable 24
Mini Cheese Muffins 22
Mini Meat Loaf with Blue Cheese and
    Bacon 59
Muffins, Apricot Buttermilk 14
Muffins, Easy Bran 16
Muffins, Mini Cheese 22
Muffins, Spinach and Feta 16
Mushrooms, Grilled Blue Cheese 50
Mussel and Bacon Pasta 64
Mussel, Prawn and Pasta Salad 54

Nectarine Buttermilk Tart 69

Omelette, Camembert 12
Orange, Baked Cheesecake 70
Oven Roasted Vegetables 59

Parmesan, Chicken 36
Pasta, Easy Mushroom and Bacon 56
Pasta, Mussel and Bacon 64
Pasta, Salami Bake 64
Pasta, Smoked Chicken and Avocado 60
Pawpaw Smoothie 10
Pears, Maple Syrup Glazed 39
Pesto Yoghurt Sauce 46
Pie, Courgette Cheese 29
Pie, Gingered Pear Sour Cream 70
Pie, Pumpkin Maple Sour Cream 76
Pizza, Basic Dough 66
Pizza, Camembert and Salami 66
Pizza, Salmon and Crème Fraîche 66
Porridge, John's Fruit and Nut 12
Potato and Cheese Bake 50
Potato Cake, served with
    Bacon and Eggs 14
Puddings, Yorkshire with Frankfurters 62
Pumpkin Maple Sour Cream Pie 76

Quiche, Impossible-to-Fail 29

Root Vegetable Mash 24

Salad, Chicken, Brie and Bacon 30
Salad, Mussel, Prawn and Pasta 54
Salad, Spinach, Seafood and Feta 52
Salad, Vietnamese Chicken 30
Salmon and Crème Fraîche Pizza 66
Salmon, Barbecued Fillet 49
Salsa, Mango and Lychee 42
Sauce, Pesto Yoghurt 46
Sauce, Simple Tartare 79
Scones, Fruit-filled Buttermilk 19
Simple Buttermilk Dressing 79
Simple Ice-cream 40
Simple Tartare Sauce 79
Smoked Chicken and Avocado Pasta 60
Smoothie, Fruit and Banana 10
Smoothie, Fruit Salad 10
Smoothie, Pawpaw 10
Smoothie, Spirulina 10
Soup, Blue Cheese and Parsnip 24
Soup, Chilled Cucumber, Avocado
    and Yoghurt 26
Sour Cream Chocolate Cake 72
Sour Cream Pie, Gingered Pear 70
Spinach and Feta Muffins 16
Spinach, Seafood and Feta Salad 52
Spirulina Smoothie 10
Spread, John's Kumara and Rosemary 79
Spread, Sundried Tomato and Feta 79
Sundried Tomato and Feta Spread 79

Tart, Nectarine Buttermilk 69
Tarts, Blue Cheese Vegetable
    and Bacon 32
Tea Cakes, Chateau Yering 74
Turkish Bread 34

Vegetables, Char-grilled 34
Vegetables, Oven Roasted 59
Vietnamese Chicken Salad 30

Yorkshire Puddings with Frankfurters 62